Quilling

To; Margaret,
The first of a few I
hope and I'll think
of you if the ideas
'came through' for a
children book. R.
from author Elisabett

Quilling

**The art
of paper
scroll work**

Elisabeth Aaron

**B T Batsford Limited
London**

First published 1976

ISBN 0 7134 3040 0

Filmset by Servis Filmsetting Limited, Manchester
Printed and bound in Great Britain by
Butler & Tanner Ltd, Frome
for the publishers B T Batsford Limited
4 Fitzhardinge Street, London W1H 0AH

Acknowledgment

I should like to thank Mary Lawrence of Heal's Books and Prints Department for suggesting this subject for a book. It is mainly through her enthusiasm and efforts at Heal's that interest in the art of quilling has been re-awakened in this country.

I would also thank The National Trust, The Lady Lever Art Gallery and the Peterborough Museum for permission to reproduce work from their collections; also Beatrice Cotton and Sheila Pettit who kindly lent work from their private collections.

My thanks to the following individuals who provided examples of work: Victoria Champion, Barbara Lewis, Jenny Goater, Avril Green, Caroline Robertson, and Herbert Scarfe who helped and advised on resin craft.

I received enthusiasm and examples of work from the following members of staff and their classes and should like to thank all those pupils whose work has helped to illustrate this book: Maureen Garland, Crispin School, Avril Green, Elmhurst Junior School, Sheila Stephenson and Gillian Seccombe, Millfield School, all in Street, Somerset; and Marian Gibb, Edgarley School, Glastonbury, Norman Webley, Weston Zoyland Junior School.

For deciphering my notes and typing the manuscript I should like to thank Carol and Avril Green, and for initial help with photography my thanks to Richard Dacy. My grateful thanks to Peter Matthews, photographic technician of Millfield School, Street, who took most of the photographs.

Elisabeth Aaron

Baltonsborough
Somerset 1975

Quilling packs are obtainable from Heal's, 196 Tottenham Court Road, London W1A IBJ.

Contents

Historical notes

If you take narrow strips of paper, wind them into coils and allow them to spring open, they can then be formed into various shapes. Gild or paint the top edges, arrange the shapes into a design which can be set on a suitable background and you have a decorative artform, resembling metal filigree. Using cream vellum on a similar background produces work with the appearance of an ivory carving. In England such work has so far been referred to as paper filigree or the art of paper rolling. The word 'quill-work' and hence the general term 'quilling' seem to be unique to America. Presumably at one time the paper was wound round quills, either those of birds or of porcupines. As the term 'quilling' is a useful one, it will be used in this book, though it will not be necessary to have a supply of quills at the ready in order to enjoy this art.

It is difficult to piece together any consecutive history of the craft. According to G B Hughes, in an article 'English Filigree Paper Work', in *Country Life* magazine 21 September 1951, such designs formed from paper were used in English churches and religious houses during the fifteenth century and until the Reformation. In 1320 the first paper mill had been established in England. It is not difficult to imagine that monks, with their knowledge of inks, paints and gilding, together with their desire to have decorative screens and panels in their churches, used paper to copy the metal filigree designs which had originated in Byzantium. Foliage, fruits, geometric patterns, scroll-work flowing and twisting its way through the design: all these may have been formed from paper, placed on edge, gilded, and so have presented to worshippers and travellers a rich, intricate magnificence of gold filigree work. There may still be panels in old churches, either here or on the Continent which close examination might reveal were made from paper. So far, although travellers have reported seeing such work, no documented evidence exists and no reproductions of this early work have been noted.

The craft appears to have been revived as a secular art in about 1660 and again in the late eighteenth century. It seems that whenever the more costly metalwork was in vogue, paper was used as a substitute.

In the first revival, it appears to have been used for making decorative panels. In days when paintings to hang on the wall were few and far between, panels of quilling were used for such decoration. Sometimes quilling was used to make a more elaborate surround for a miniature. Two existing examples from that time show quilling used to make elaborate backgrounds for wax figures, the rolled paper forming the dress and the curtaining in the background.

Later, it became a craft for young ladies of leisure. In the *New Lady's Magazine*, 1786, describing filigree work as 'an art to be pursued at a very trifling expense', a series of twelve sheets of patterns was issued. In 1791, the Princess Elizabeth was supplied with 'fifteen ounces of different filigree papers, one ounce of gold paper and a box made for filigree work with ebony moulding, lock and key, lined inside and outside'. The *Gentleman's Magazine* of that time describes the well finished boxes, usually octagonal or hexagonal in shape, being decorated by young ladies. The boxes had a deep depression in each of their sides, to be filled with designs made from 3 mm ($\frac{1}{8}$ in.) strips of paper. Miniatures of a house or of a screen were often the centrepieces of the boxes, around which scrolls and patterns were worked. In Jane Austen's novel *Sense and Sensibility*, Eleanor Dashwood offered to 'roll papers' for Lucy Steel who was making a filigree basket.

At that time, also, the craft became a pastime for the French Napoleonic prisoners of war. These men left a superb record of 'crafts for little cost'. Straw from their palliasses was used in marquetry, bones became intricately carved ships and models and paper was used for filigree work. Just as elegant cabinets can be found which have doors, drawers, and even legs, covered with straw marquetry, so at least one cabinet, now in The Lady Lever Gallery, exists, which is decorated in paper filigree.

In America the craft appears to have been used mainly as a decoration on sconces — ornaments for carrying candles. Various coloured papers were used, coated with wax and sprinkled with bits of glass to catch the light of the candles.

There are examples of this craft still to be found in museums: tea caddies, wine coasters and pictures. In several cases the paper was arranged in festoons or wreaths around a central panel, a medallion, a miniature or a motif made from another material, such as a spray of waxed flowers. Trays, picture frames, ink stands were all at some time used as a base on which to arrange these paper shapes.

At a local arts and crafts exhibition I put on a display of quilling and asked if anyone had ever come across any examples. A quilled tea caddy in the seemingly traditional hexagonal form of the early nineteenth century was thus discovered in the next village. The caddy is in a very good state of preservation and I have been able to restore the parts which had a few scrolls missing.

Today the craft may be seeing another revival. It has the advantages of being cheap, requiring no special tools, and of suiting the whole age range from seven to ninetyseven!

A wax portrait of Queen Anne, *c* 1710 *Reproduced by courtesy of The Lady Lever Art Gallery*

Late eighteenth-century cabinet-on-stand, with
printed medallions surrounded by designs in rolled
paper *Reproduced by courtesy of The Lady Lever
Art Gallery*

Tea caddy
Reputed to be the work of Napoleonic prisoners of
war of the late eighteenth-early nineteenth centuries

Tea caddy
18 × 11 × 14 cm high ($7\frac{1}{4} \times 4\frac{1}{4} \times 5\frac{1}{2}$ in.)
Gilded brownish paper scrolls with a pale turquoise
to the star on the lid. The background to the sides
is crushed mother of pearl with a little sand.
The design of trees in the front oval is gilt on black
Private Collection

Tea caddy
18 × 11 × 14 cm high (7¼ × 4¼ × 5½ in.)
A background of black scrolls with the design
entirely in strongly gilded paper. The pictures of
houses on the front and back are pale brown
etchings with the roofs in blue-grey

Private Collection

Overleaf:
Paper work panel surrounding a portrait of a child
in wax, 1702   *Reproduced by courtesy of The
Lady Lever Art Gallery*

Basket of flowers in bright shades of blue, yellow,
orange and brown on a mother of pearl background.
Diameter 19 cm (7½ in.)   *Reproduced by courtesy*
of The Peterborough Museum

Wine coaster
Diameter 12 cm (5 in.)   *Reproduced by courtesy*
of The Peterborough Museum

The Blackett coat of arms, prior to 1777 19
42 × 34 cm (16½ × 13½ in.)
Gild scrolls on a red centre background with a
white background to the surround
Wallington Hall, Northumberland   *Reproduced by*
kind permission of The National Trust

Left:
Tea caddy   *Private Collection*

Below left:
Restoring damaged panel

Details of panels

Materials

Paper

Paper for quilling should be firm enough to hold its shape yet sufficiently lightweight to be rolled smoothly either on a tool or by itself.

Most types of paper, and even thin card, can be used to help give different effects and from a box of 'offcuts' creative forms of all kinds can be produced. Coloured tissue paper is useful as fillers for the centres of flowers: thin card makes firm, open shapes such as hearts and cartridge paper can be used for any of the basic shapes. Any small lengths are useable — minute scrolls can be formed from a short left over strip.

Traditionally, the quilling seems to have been worked with 3 mm ($\frac{1}{8}$ in.) strips. This is a useful width, giving some depth and three-dimensional effect and yet not too bulky for jewellery and for setting the object under glass. Do, however, quill with wider strips or try even narrower ones if you are nimble fingered. Some of the examples shown are by young children using strips up to 25 mm (1 in.) wide. Any wider than this the shapes will tend to collapse.

A guillotine or photo trimmer is useful for cutting a great number of strips quickly though difficulty may be found in producing strips of much less than 6 mm ($\frac{1}{4}$ in.). Hand cutting is laborious but will provide enough strips for an individual's needs. A sharp knife, steel rule and wooden board are required.

Alternatively, if you have a friendly local printer, he may be pleased to get rid of his trimmings or he may even be prevailed upon to cut some strips for you, perhaps in return for a picture made by you from his 'waste'. There should also be a quilling pack on the market.

Coloured paper can obviously be used to good effect or the paper can be coloured before cutting. Aerosol cans are now available containing gold, silver and most other colours. On the other hand, the quilled object may be sprayed after it is made up. This is more wasteful but the spray does act as an additional adhesive if it is used after all the shapes are glued together. Some very pleasing effects are obtainable by just touching the edges with paint — for example, on mobiles which turn in the breeze, a two colour effect is produced.

Hand cutting strips of paper

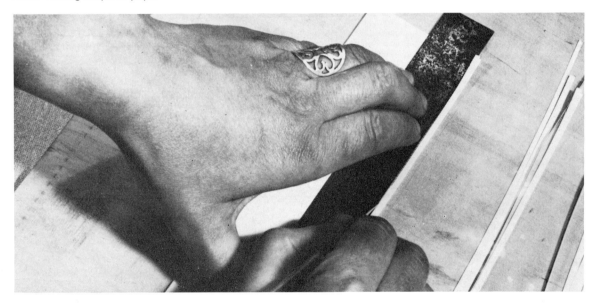

Glue

I have found the best glue to be any of the white, rubbery type adhesives. They dry very quickly and do not trail lengths of of glue over the work as do the impact adhesives. You may, however, find the latter more useful when it comes to attaching the work to the final surface. Household cement glues or epoxy resins should be used in jewellery making to fix the quilling to a metal pin or backing.

A cocktail stick is a useful tool for applying the glue as only very small amounts are needed. If the stick is kept stuck in a damp sponge, it should keep clean. A sheet of waxed paper makes an excellent working surface as the shapes being glued together will not stick to it.

Tools

As for quilling tools, just take a look around — especially into that fruit bowl which holds everything but fruit! A cocktail stick, a darning or knitting needle, a pencil (*not* screwdrivers — the tight coil won't come off the end); any of these will do fine. You can make your own quilling tool by either filing off the end of the eye of a needle or by cutting a small slit in the end of a dowel rod. The paper is then slotted in and can be more quickly wound.

Aids

To produce even-sized coils is very difficult, especially for the beginner. So, take another look in that fruit bowl or the kitchen drawer and find some rings: curtain rings, small lids, washers, etc. When a coil has been wound, it can be placed in a ring, will expand to fill it, and can then be glued and more of the same size made.

A ruler, pencil and scissors may be needed at some stage and if you have a pair of tweezers, you will find them very helpful. So far, nothing special has been bought, just some imagination used!

Further decoration
Beads and sequins are useful weight
increasers for pendants and earrings and
add a further sparkle to decorated boxes,
but use them sparingly.

Now to quilling . . .

Instructions

Coils

To begin any coil, take the end of a strip of paper and wind it tightly on to your quilling tool for a round or two. Then, by rotating the tool and quilling the paper so that each round sits on top of the last, a coil will be formed. If your tool has a small slit at the top, the end of the paper should be caught in this and the same procedure followed. In order to remove the coil from the tool, twist the tool slightly in the opposite direction from the way you have been winding.

Open forms
Open forms using 102 mm (4 in.) for practice.

Loose open coil
Form a coil but stop winding about 25 mm (1 in.) from the end of the strip. The coil is allowed to spring open and left unglued.

Open heart
Fold a strip in half and make a small crease. Wind each end of the strip towards the centre. The coils are allowed to spring apart and left unglued or glued sparingly where the coils touch.

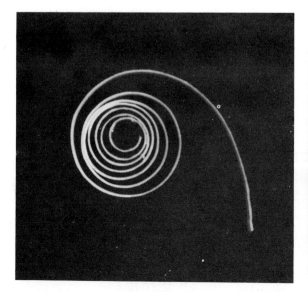

V-shape
This is the same as for the heart but each side is wound away from the crease

'S'-shape
Wind one end of the strip to just past the centre, release, turn the strip and wind the other end to just past the centre, release

Scroll
Wind one end of the strip towards the centre, release, roll the other end towards the centre, release

Closed forms
Closed forms using 25 cm (10 in.) for practice — glue will be needed.

Tight coil or filler
Wind the strip all the way to the end, remove it from the tool and glue the end to hold the shape

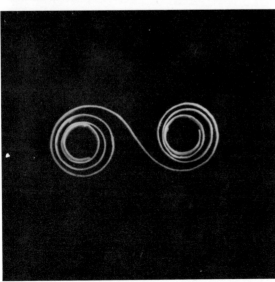

Large tight coil
Wind the strip on to a large tool such as a dowel rod and glue the end. As long as the coil can easily be removed, it is often better to glue it while it is on the tool. This basic shape can be further formed into petals, etc

Loose closed coil
Wind the strip right to the end, but before gluing, allow the coil to expand to the desired size

Pear drop
Make a loose coil and, after gluing, pinch one side to a point, trying to make the glued end part of the point

Eye
Follow the directions for making the pear drop, turn the drop round and pinch the opposite end to form an eye

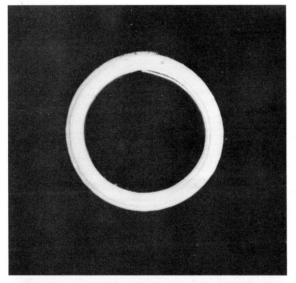

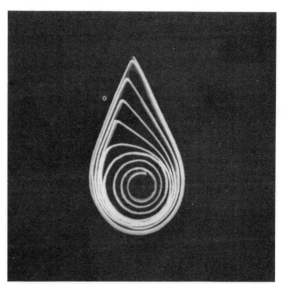

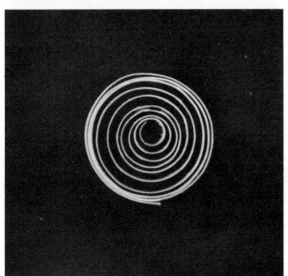

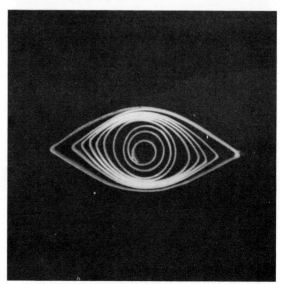

Leaf shape
Follow the directions for making an eye
but as you pinch the opposite ends, shape
the coil gently to form a leaf

Petal shape
Follow the directions for making a pear
drop and as you pinch one end, shape the
piece gently to form a petal

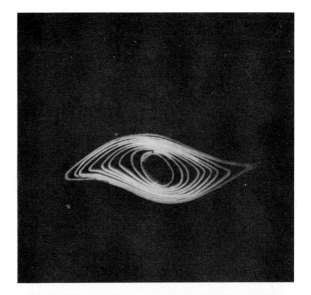

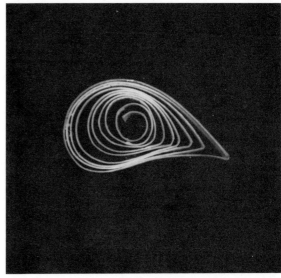

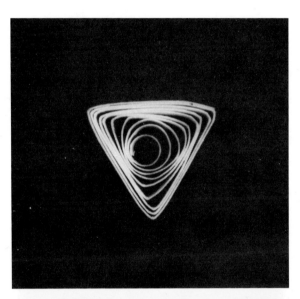

Triangle
Follow the directions for making a loose coil, then gently squeeze the shape into a triangular form, pinching the corners to retain the shape

Semi-circle
Follow the directions for making a loose coil, then gently squeeze into a semi-circle, pinching the two points to retain the shape

These are the basic forms necessary for the examples given in this book — many others may be invented.

Starting coil

Technique
Simple examples to make

Closed forms
Closed forms using a cocktail stick
(a) Make 6 eyes using 279 mm (11 in.)
(b) Make 6 loose (closed) coils using
     140 mm (5½ in.)
(c) Make 12 pear drops using 140 mm
     (5½ in.)

Glue the 6 eyes together as shown, then
glue the loose coils into the gaps between
the eyes. Finally, glue the pear drops to
the tops of the eyes.

Winding complete

Coil placed in ring

Glue applied to end of strip

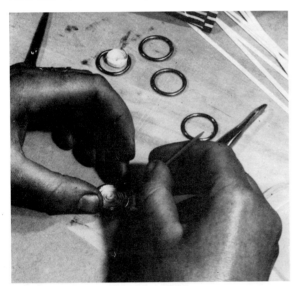

Glued join held with tweezers

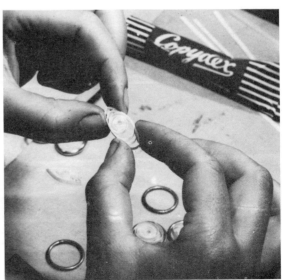

Shape formed

'Eye' formed

Gluing two shapes together

Gluing whole design

Design glued onto background

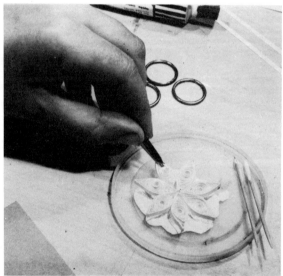

This example could be used as a wine coaster after being sprayed: on a smaller scale, it could be used as a pendant

See completed work overleaf.

Different arrangements of
similar shapes

Open forms

Open forms using a cocktail stick
(a) Make 3 loose open coils using
    127 mm (5 in.)
(b) Make 6 loose open coils using 64 mm
    (2½ in.)
(c) Make 3 loose open coils using 25 mm
    (1 in.)
When the coils have all been made, glue
the end of one of the 64 mm (2½ in.)
coils and stick a 25 mm (1 in.) coil to it
on the same side. On the opposite side,
glue the end of a 127 mm (5 in.) coil.
The stem of the spray will gradually be
formed as you work downwards, arranging
the coils as shown.

Worked examples

Branch with leaves

1 Make 18 leaf shapes using 279 mm (11 in.)
Some of the leaves can be made by
joining different coloured strips together
to give a darker effect inside or outside
2 Make branch by pulling strips of card
over the edge of a ruler — this will give
the curved effect. Lengths of curved card
are then stuck together to form a branch.
Glue the leaves along the branch

Butterfly

(a) make 2 pear drops using 46 cm (18 in.)
(b) make 2 pear drops using 30 cm (12 in.)
(c) make 2 pear drops using 254 mm (10 in.)
(d) Make 2 pear drops using 76 mm (3 in.)
(e) Make 1 squashed loose closed coil
using 30 cm (12 in.)
(f) Make 2 loose open coils using 254 mm
(1 in.)

Bring b, c and d together with glue to
form lower wings. Glue (a) to lower wings
and attach (f) to form antennae

Dragon fly (top right on page 43)

(a) Make 4 petal shapes using 30 cm
(12 in.)
(b) Make 1 loose closed coil using 254 mm
(10 in.)
(c) Make 4 (or more) loose coils using
50 mm (2 in.)

(b) forms the body, though in this case it
has been pushed into a head and body
shape. The wings (a) have been flattened
at the end to give a firm join to the body.
The coils made in (c) are then joined to
form the long body and a small 'u' shaped
piece of paper is added to form the tail

Open forms in a rectangle

Variations on the theme of open forms

Rose design

(a) Make 1 tight coil using 30 cm (12 in.)
(b) Make 8 scrolls using 25 mm (1 in.)
(c) Make 8 scrolls using 38 mm (1½ in.)
(d) Make 24 scrolls using 38 mm (1½ in.)

Glue (b) around (a), then (c) around the outside. 8 of the scrolls formed in (d) are then added, leaving a small gap between each one. A strip of 30 cm (12 in.) is then wrapped round this form and glued and the rest of the scrolls formed in (d) stuck round the outside

Fly

(a) Make 2 pear drops using 30 cm (12 in.)
(b) Make 1 pear drop using 203 mm (8 in.)
(c) Make 1 tight coil using 50 mm (2 in.)
(d) Make 1 pair legs from 50 mm (2 in.)

The two large pear drops are stuck to (b) as shown, leaving a space for the head and tops of legs which are then glued into place

Butterfly

(a) Make 2 large tight coils using 46 cm (18 in.) – shape into wings
(b) Make 3 large tight coils using 254 mm (10 in.) – shape one into body and two into lower wings
(c) Make 2 pear drops using 254 mm (10 in.)
(d) Make 16 open coils using 25 mm (1 in.)
(e) Make 2 open coils using 25 mm (1 in.)

Glue (c) and (d) into wings as shown. Stick wings and body together and add (e) to form antennae

(b) and (c) are glued into (a), then (a) and (d) are brought together alternately. (e) is glued on to the top. For added decoration, small strips of coloured paper can be stuck under (e) before it is finally stuck down, to form a more frilly centre

Flowers

1 Zigzag flower

(a) Make tight coil using 50 cm (20 in.) Two strips of dark paper have been added to this to form a contrast at the centre and at the edge

(b) Make 12 tight coils using 76 mm (3 in.) Arrange (b) around (a), add a zigzag arrangement made by folding paper like a concertina, using 254 mm (10 in.)

2 Flower

(a) Make 1 tight coil using 50 cm (20 in.) surrounded by contrast colour strip, 254 mm (10 in.)

(b) Make length of small zigzag and stick this around tight coils 127 mm (5 in.)

(c) Make 12 leaf shapes using 254 mm (10 in.)

Stick petals together then place (a) plus (b) on top of petals. The centre has been pushed down

3 Large flower

(a) Make 6 large tight coils using 50 cm (20 in.) — shape into petals

(b) Make 6 eyes using 254 mm (10 in.)

(c) Make 12 eyes using 254 mm (10 in.)

(d) Make 6 eyes using 254 mm (10 in.)

(e) Make 1 tight coil with 50 cm (20 in.) with 254 mm (10 in.) coloured strip

4 Flower

(a) Make 7 large tight coils, form into petal shape 50 cm (20 in.)

(b) Make 7 pear drops using 152 mm (6 in.)

Stick (b) into (a), then the petals are stuck together

5 Small flower

(a) Make 5 large tight coils using 254 mm (10 in.) — form them into petals

(b) Make 1 tight coil using 50 cm (20 in.) surrounded by a further 254 mm (10 in.) of contrasting colour

Stick petals together, then stick (b) on top of petals. The centre has been pushed down to form a deep centre to the flower

Development of ideas

Doodling

Doodling with quilling can produce a whole range of animals and birds

Borders

Striking borders can be formed from either open or closed forms. These can be used on lamp shades, photoframes or round a quilled picture.

Have a closer look at some of the pictorial examples from some fine borders

Corners

Arrangements of both open and closed forms can be used to make corners for pictures, table mats and trays

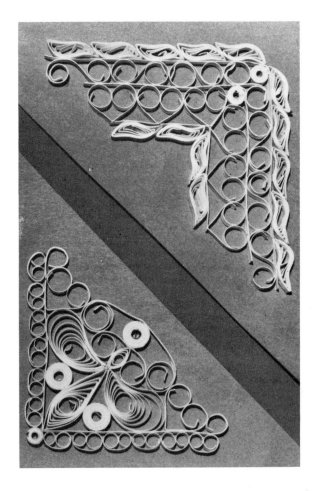

Doodling

Borders

Abstract arrangements

You will find that arrangements just grow
or ideas come from seeing a haphazard
arrangement of shapes previously quilled
and not used

Quilling designs using pins

A slightly different design can be made
by using pins to hold the strips in place.
Metal filigree is worked in this way.
Several examples of this sort of design
can be seen on the historical examples

These pages of basic design and several worked examples form the nucleus of the craft. Practice obviously makes perfect but you should soon be quilling with some speed.

The rest of the book is devoted to the use of quilling in a practical way. No specific instructions have been given since all the basic shapes have already been described. While learning to quill, it is quite amazing how you see quilled shapes all around — the wallpaper, the floor tiles, door handles, the curtains, wrought-iron work. Keep these designs in mind or jot them down — they may come in useful. You may also glean ideas for designs from embroidery transfers.

Quilling with more than one strip at a time

If the ends of several strips are joined together, either exactly on top of each other or in a slightly tapering manner, the strips can all be coiled together. When the coil has been allowed to spring open, the loose ends can be quilled separately. Alternatively, the strips can be glued together at their centre and then either end of each strip quilled

Jewellery

Pendants, brooches, earrings, even elaborate necklaces, can be formed by quilling.

It is necessary, in most cases, to use metal attachments if the jewellery is to be wearable. If you live in a large town, you may be able to buy jewellery 'bits and pieces' from a handicraft shop. Otherwise, it is fairly straightforward to order by post from a handicraft supplier. It is useful to know the different terms involved:

Findings

Findings the general term for metallic bits and pieces, usually applied to earrings.

Bell caps these fit on the top of earrings allowing them to be hung from ear wires, screws or clips or enabling a pendant to be attached to a chain or leather thonging.

Ear wire finding for pierced ears.

Bar-screw finding for non-pierced ears.

Jump rings allow the bell-capped pendants to be hung from chains or thongings. They can also be used to link quilled shapes together.

Bolt ring is the fastening device for the end of a chain to be used in conjunction with a jump ring.

Leather thonging, chains or Russian braid can be purchased from suppliers as well as pendant blanks with chains already attached.

Bell caps

Jump rings   Bolt ring

Ear wire   Ear screw
with loop   with loop

Small   Bar pin
oval pin

Quilling on cloth covered cardboard

The back is then covered with another, smaller, piece of neatened material.
The centre part of a cord 80 cm (33 in.) in length is sewn round the outside edge and the remaining lengths knotted at the end

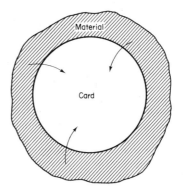

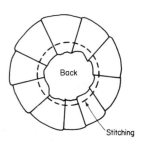

Quilled shapes linked by jump rings. The metallic top is the inside of an empty well cleaned tooth paste tube, the holes being made with a leather punch. It is mounted on a bar pin

Quilling mounted on copper blanks. The copper may be left plain though it will retain a better metallic colour if sprayed with clear polyurethane. An aerosol spray of enamel paint can be used to good effect, either on the blank or on the copper together with its quilling

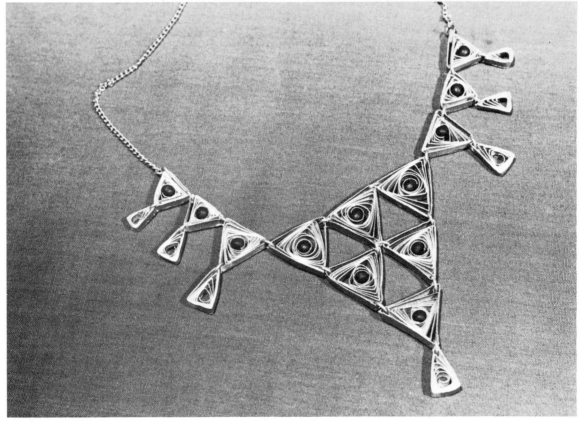

Top left:
An elaborate necklace

Bottom left:
Quilled triangles

Right:
Brooches mounted

Below:
Earrings

Chokers — quilling mounted on suede. The upper one is fastened by thongs, the lower one by Velcro. Although velvet is a pleasing material to use for chokers, the pile makes it difficult to attach the quilling successfully

Pendant with background of fabric covered card

Large pendant with background made from an
offcut of leather

Pendant with background made from the lid of a
drum of bicarbonate of soda

Pendant with background made from an offcut of suede

Mobiles

In 1930, Alexander Calder took inspiration from the hanging chandeliers which had been known since the early 1600s and evolved a new art form — moving sculpture or mobiles.

The main idea of the mobile is to give visual pleasure; the parts making up the whole should hang freely to catch small currents of air. Quilling lends itself to the making of mobiles, either to hang singly or to be suspended in groups. Wire, cane, straw or straws slotted with wire can be used as arms on which to hang the threaded shapes.

It is often time consuming to adjust the mobile so that it is perfectly balanced, the shapes so hanging that they do not catch on each other when turning. Once balance has been achieved, the thread used in the hanging can be glued in place on the wire or cane, acting as the arms.

Mobile made by a group of 13-year olds. Twisted wire has been used here as a support as the hanging forms varied greatly in weight

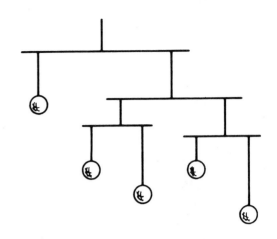

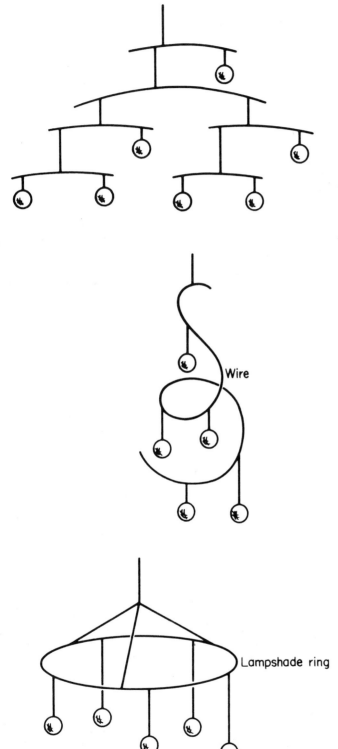

Wire

Lampshade ring

The sun with the moving face. The cardboard circle
was formed round a tin and left on the tin while
the outer decoration was glued on

A single butterfly mobile

The rim of a plastic lid makes an ideal setting for quilled shapes. The rim may be left as it is or sprayed

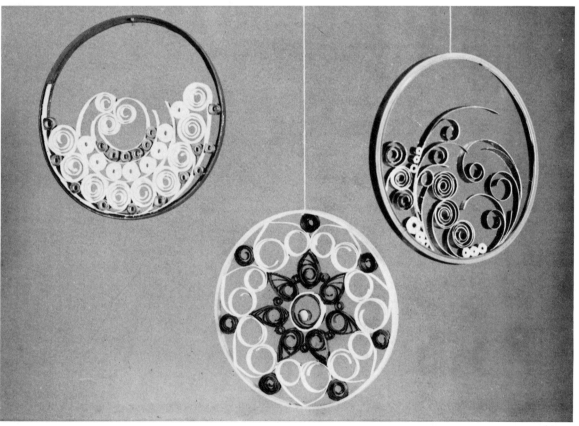

Sun shape

Christmas

If you are always on the look out for new ideas in Christmas tree decorations, cards, and gift decorations, quilling should provide you with some inspiration.

A paper Christmas tree formed from many loose open coils, varying in length 127 mm (5 in.) to 38 mm ($1\frac{1}{2}$ in.). The coils have been stuck, beginning at the bottom, on 6 mm ($\frac{1}{4}$ in.) dowel rod which fits nicely into a cotton reel which then acts as the base

A three-dimensional golden lily for a Christmas table decoration

Gift decorations. In two of these, the head of a dried flower has been incorporated with the quilling

A regal crown for a wise man in the Nativity
play and a jewelled box for him to carry

Christmas cards

Angels

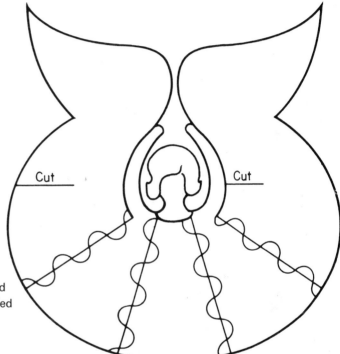

The pattern for the angels
The angel can be cut paper. It is then bent round
and the two cuts slotted into each other. A quilled
design can then be stuck on to give a rich
decoration to her dress and wings

Christmas tree decorations

Printing and stencilling

Printing

Quilled shapes make excellent printing motifs on paper or cloth. The most important requirement is that the strips are of completely equal width.

The quilled design is stuck very firmly on a thick piece of card. It is important that all parts of the design are stuck — any movement will spoil the result.

The top of the design is then covered with printing ink by means of a roller, if available, then pressed down where the print is required. I have found it best to use oil-based printing ink since the water based ones tend to make the quilled design rather soggy and it loses its definition.

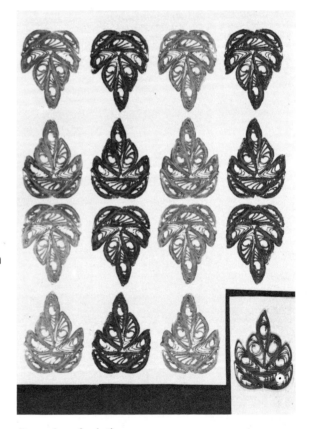

Examples of printing

Quilled design

A more complicated printed pattern

A print from the quilled design

Left:
Printing on material

Below:
Stencilling

The openness of quilling lends itself to stencilling using a paint spray

A simple design has been sprayed

The first design is covered

The design is held in place with a cocktail stick whilst being sprayed

The design is held until paint is dry

An overall design can be built up

Pictures and cards

Pictures

The more one quills, the more one realizes how versatile the craft is. If you are wanting a wall hanging, a picture or a card for a special occasion, I am sure you will be able to build it up from the basic quilled shapes.

I have found that the best material on which to mount pictures is good cotton. You can buy it in a lovely range of colours which adds texture to a picture but does not interfere with the clear outlines of the quilling. Do not glue the material on to the mounting card but rather glue the wrap-around at the back of the card.

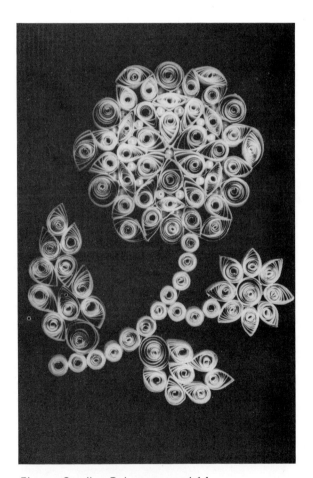

Flower Caroline Robertson aged 14

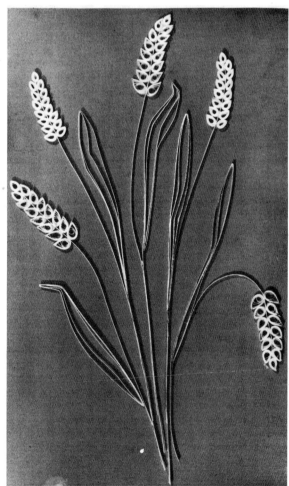

Crinoline Lady Avril Green

Wheat Top edge sprayed gold on olive green
backing

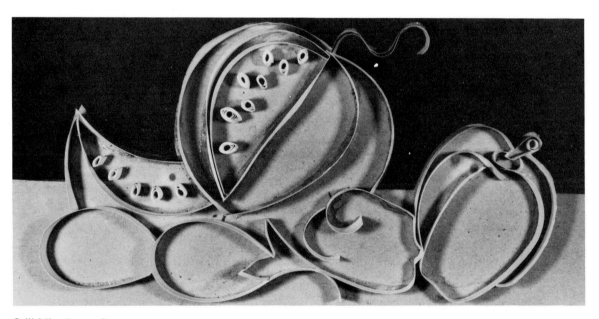

Still Life Jenny Goater

Butterflies and creeping plant Golden butterflies,
white plant on lilac backing

Valentine, incorporating some nylon edging

Easter cards and Best Wishes cards

Quilling on objects

Boxes

Quilling can make a decorative finish to such objects as boxes, table mats, teapot stands, mirrors, tray and lampshades.

Those pleasing boxes that one hesitates to throw away; visiting card boxes, sugar boxes, some wooden cheese containers, can be decorated with quilling to become a charming jewel box on a dressing table. Gold or silver sprays can be used either on the box alone or on the box with the quilling attached.

Wooden boxes look well left as they are though a coat or two of matt polyurethane would help to keep them clean. If they are to be sprayed with paint, wooden boxes need a good rub down with wire wool or fine sandpaper.

Table mats and coasters

Quilled designs where the work fits fairly tightly together as in the first closed form worked example given (page 39) can be sprayed with polyurethane or paint and used as wine coasters.

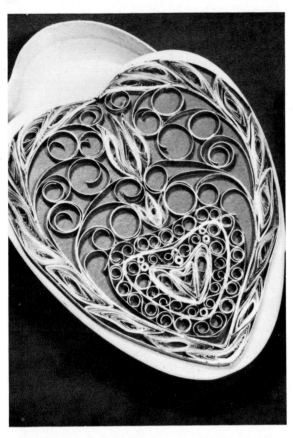

Left:
A white wood box

Below:
Two visiting card boxes

Opposite top:
A cloth-covered jewellery box

Opposite bottom:
Selection of work by Caroline Robertson

Left:
A quilled top for a plain
white wood box

The mirror on the left had a very plain perspex
frame. The right hand mirror was made from a
mirror bathroom tile stuck with its own adhesive
to a piece of plywood

Lampshade with quilled edging

A decorative cross. A strip of wood 6 mm ($\frac{1}{4}$ in.)
by 12 mm ($\frac{1}{2}$ in.) has been used to make the arms
of the cross: the quilling was made with 6 mm
($\frac{1}{4}$ in.) wide strips

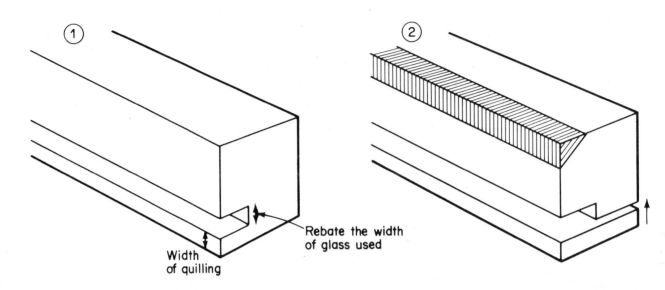

① Width
of quilling

Rebate the width
of glass used

②

Bottom left:

This tray provides an example of setting the quilling under glass to give it protection. I used 6 mm ($\frac{1}{4}$ in.) plate glass for the tray but for a picture a lighter weight sheet of glass should be used

In (1) a rebate has been cut to hold the glass. If you do not have recourse to a rebating tool, you could saw or chisel out the L shaped part and then glue or tack on the extra piece, as shown in (2) to form a rebate.

The shaded part could be planed off to make a lighter frame. When making the picture or tray base, you must remember to allow for the width of the frame all round. The final step is to glue or tack the plywood or hardboard mounted picture or tray base to the frame

Below:

A quilled design set between two pieces of perspex to make a table mat or teapot stand. The upper and lower perspex sheets are kept apart by thin strips of wood the same width as that of the quilling, in this case 6 mm ($\frac{1}{4}$ in.). The perspex was sawed with a hacksaw blade and *Uhu* glue used

Resin work

A quilled design will be made much more permanent if set in resin. Kits for resin craft may be bought in most toy shops and contain clear instructions, moulds and the necessary chemicals. The resin is supplied in liquid form and, after adding a few drops of hardener, it soon becomes a hard, transparent substance, looking like clear glass. The article to be embedded is placed in a mould and covered by the resin before the hardening process begins. It is easily removed from the mould after a few hours and can then be polished.

When setting quilling there are two or three points to be watched. (a) It is much simpler to make the quilling to fit an existing mould than to try to find a suitable mould afterwards. (b) Some metallic paints will not embed in resin satisfactorily: for example, gold metallic paint tends to darken and also come off the paper, so discolouring the resin. (c) If your design is made from very light paper, it may tend to float in the resin and so the instructions for less dense items should be carefully followed.

Above right:
Paper weights

Finger plate and door knob

Below right:
Pendant and ring mounts

Children's work

This section contains work by 7 to 14 year
olds, mainly in a class room situation.
Quilled shapes seem to appeal to the
imagination of the child. For those who
are not confident in drawing, a whole
array of flower petals, butterfly wings and
shapes for patterns are formed quite
simply. Meanwhile, a whole new art
form is available for the teacher.

Portrait

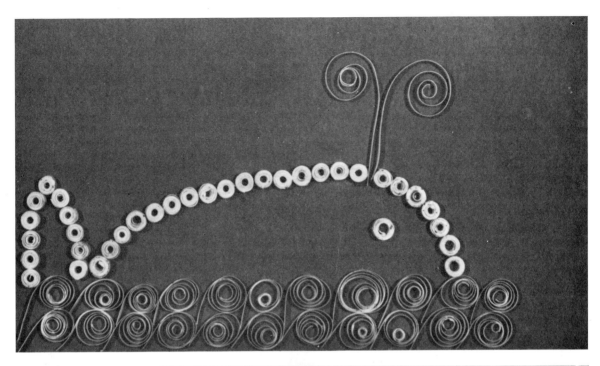

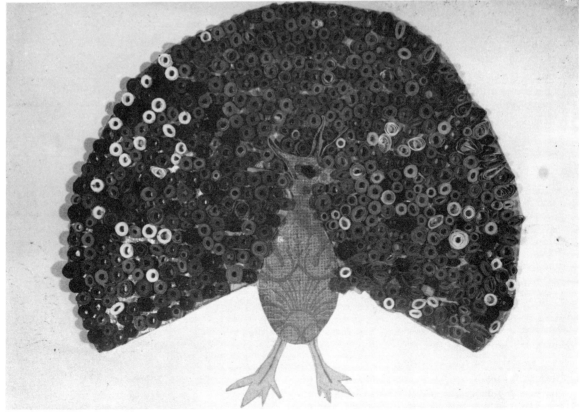

Top left:
Whale

Bottom left:
Peacock

Right:
Butterfly

Below:
Duck

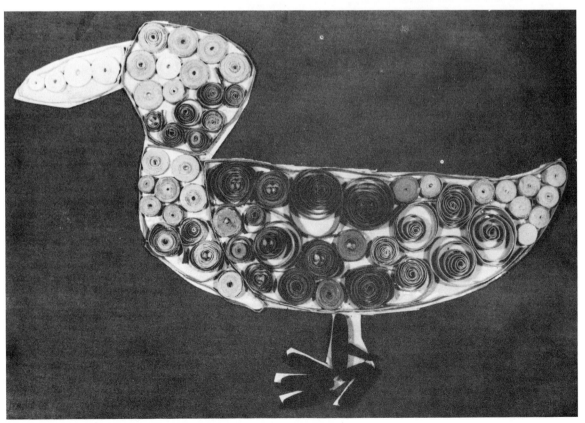

Opposite:
Dragon

Pages 108–109
A class effort by 10 and 11 year olds
91 cm x 137 cm (3 ft x 4 ft 6 in.)

Pendants in lids

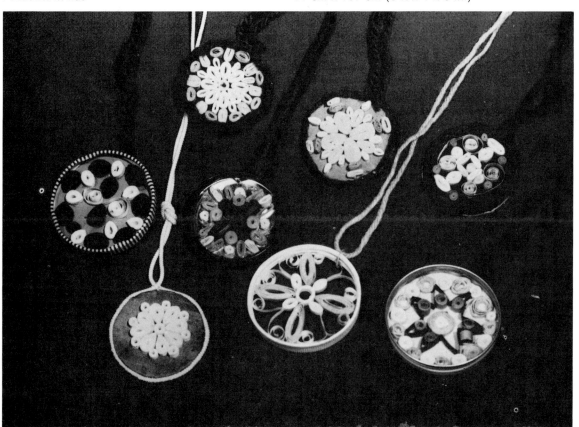

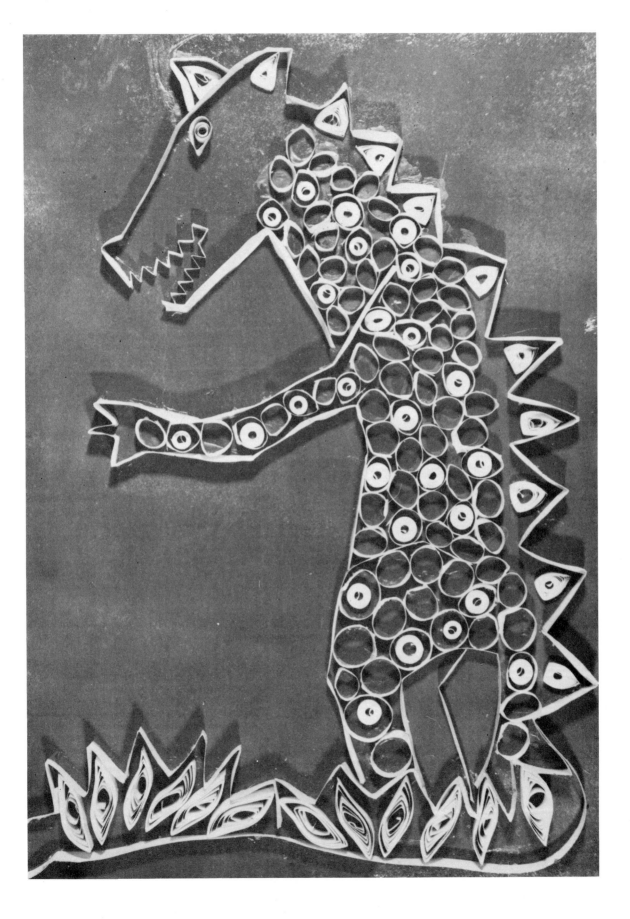

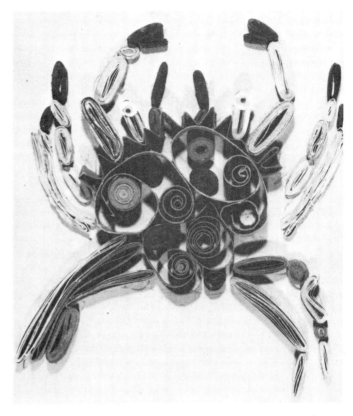

Right:
Crab

Below:
Bird

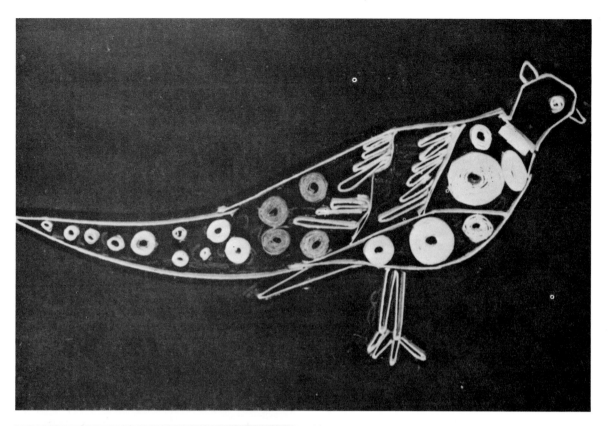

Above:
Pheasant

Left:
Face

Quilling
with other materials

The basic technique of quilling may be applied successfully to other materials such as straw, wood, cane, corrugated paper, string, leather or hessian, provided the material can be prepared in strips.

Straw
Lengths of natural straw can be split open, ironed flat and present a challenging quilling material. The grain of the straw makes for difficulty in rolling tightly but if the straw is dampened with water this helps to avoid cracking.

Wood
Ready made coils can be picked up from the floor of the carpenter's workshop: use them to make a textured picture.

Pendant made from leather thonging

Flowers made from thin waxed string. The idea of
11 year old Mark Stacey after seeing paper quilling

Horse's head in wood shavings by Charles Pearson

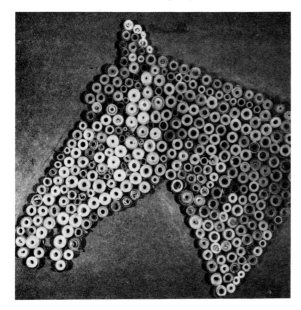

Paper necklace and bracelet Long, tapering pieces
of paper are needed to make the beads — colour
supplement advertisements make colourful ones.
They should measure 25 mm (1 in.) at one end,
tapering to a point at the other and should be about
30 cm (12 in.) long. Starting at the wide end, the
strips are wound tightly. The tapering end is well
stuck down. The beads can then be threaded on
bead elastic

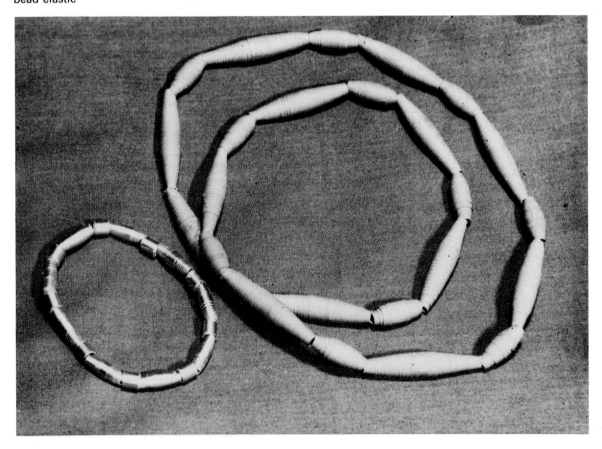

Lengths of hessian made into large coils — the idea
of 11 year old Caroline Peeters

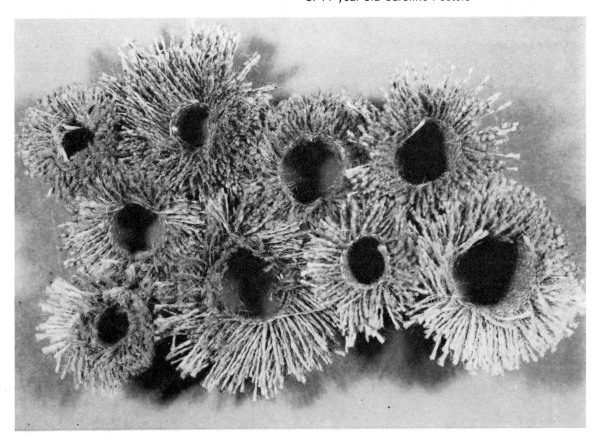

Paper city Quilling with varying widths of cartridge paper.
The paper is wound along a dowel rod rather than the usual way so that cone shapes are formed

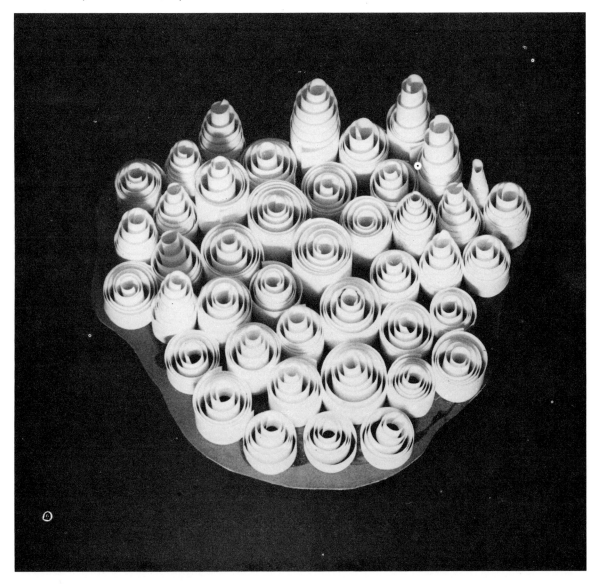

An idea for quilling in cane from the hair slides
made in Asia

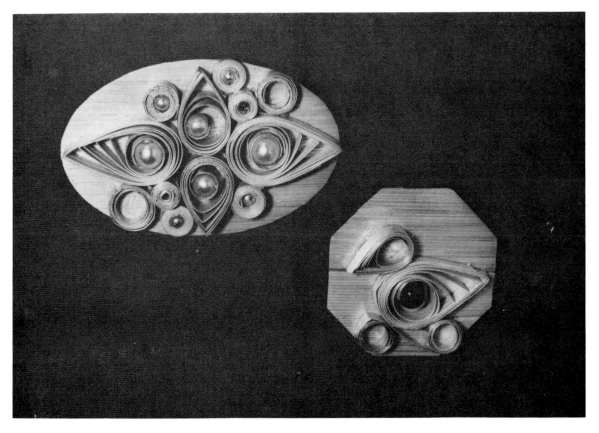

Two straw brooches, the quilled shapes mounted
on a background of flattened straw

Coils of corrugated paper, glued together and
sprayed make a useful teapot stand